Contents

Preface 3

Introduction 4

Chapter 1: 8

Chapter 2: 9

Chapter 3: 11

Chapter 4: 13

Chapter 5: 16

Chapter 6: 18

Chapter 7: 19

Chapter 8: 21

Chapter 9: 23

Chapter 10: 25

Conclusion 30

Glossary 31

Preface

The maritime and offshore industries are facing transformative times, with rapid advancements in technology, stricter regulatory frameworks, and an ever-growing need for enhanced operational safety and compliance. Recognizing the need for practical, accessible, and targeted knowledge, the Gosships Learning Series was created to offer industry professionals the tools they need to stay ahead of these changes.

This series is designed to provide foundational to intermediate knowledge, with a focus on practical application and real-world relevance. Each book in the series is coupled with a certification test, ensuring that the knowledge gained is not only understood but can also be effectively applied in professional settings.

The Gosships Learning Series is meant to empower maritime and energy sector personnel, from entry-level crew members to shoreside managers, by equipping them with the skills needed to navigate the complexities of modern operations. We hope this series will support your professional development and open new opportunities for growth and success in your career.

Introduction

Welcome to the Gosships Learning Series, designed for professionals looking to expand their knowledge and enhance their careers in the maritime and energy sectors. This book, titled "Hydrogen: The Fuel of the Future", was meticulously crafted by experienced regulators and industry executives, ensuring that the content is both authoritative and aligned with current industry standards. Whether you're new to the topic or seeking to deepen your expertise, this resource is tailored to give you the insights you need to sound like an expert among your peers.

In this book, we will explore the following key areas:

- Hydrogen Production Methods: Learn about electrolysis, steam methane reforming, and emerging technologies.

- Hydrogen Storage and Transport: Understand the challenges and solutions for storing and transporting hydrogen safely.

- Applications of Hydrogen: Discover how hydrogen is used in transportation, industry, and power generation.

- Environmental and Economic Considerations: Explore the economic viability of hydrogen and its role in decarbonizing industries.

- Hydrogen Safety: Dive into safety protocols and advancements to ensure hydrogen is handled securely.

After reading this book, you will be ready to take an assessment designed to test your comprehension of the material. Upon successful completion of the assessment, you can obtain a Certificate of Achievement by visiting www.gosships.com

and accessing the training platform. This certificate validates your expertise in this critical area and helps demonstrate your proficiency to industry peers.

Who is this book for?

This book is designed for:

- Maritime and offshore personnel seeking to improve their knowledge.

- Shoreside managers looking to enhance their understanding of industry best practices.

- Aspiring students aiming to break into the industry with a solid foundation.

- Government and regulatory personnel looking to stay informed about evolving industry standards.

By mastering the concepts in this book, you'll be equipped to meet the challenges of modern operations, stay compliant with international regulations, and contribute to a safer, more efficient work environment.

Thank you for choosing the Gosships Learning Series to support your journey of continuous learning and professional growth.

Gosships Learning Series 2024/2025

1. Hydrogen: The Fuel of the Future
2. Green Ammonia: The Next Big Thing in Shipping
3. Decarbonizing Shipping: Pathways to Zero Emissions
4. Battery Technology for Industrial Applications
5. Carbon Capture and Storage: Can It Save the Planet?
6. Biofuels 101: Turning Waste into Energy
7. Understanding LNG (Liquefied Natural Gas)
8. Methanol as a Marine Fuel
9. Offshore Wind Energy: The Future of Renewable Power
10. Tidal and Wave Energy: Harnessing the Ocean
11. Electrofuels: The Next Generation of Carbon-Neutral Fuels
12. Energy Storage Systems for Grid Reliability
13. Hydrogen Fuel Cells for Transportation
14. Solar Energy Innovations: Beyond Solar Panels
15. Smart Grids: The Backbone of Future Energy Systems
16. Ammonia-Hydrogen Blends: A Dual Fuel Solution?
17. Nuclear Power: Small Modular Reactors for a Low-Carbon Future
18. Hydropower: The Oldest Renewable Energy Source
19. Decentralized Energy Systems: Microgrids for Resilience
20. Energy Efficiency Technologies for Industry
21. Hydrogen Production from Seawater
22. Fuel Cells for Maritime Applications
23. Geothermal Energy: Unlocking Earth's Heat
24. Future of EV Charging Infrastructure
25. Synthetic Fuels: Bridging the Gap to Decarbonization
26. Cybersecurity for Maritime and Offshore Operations
27. AI and Automation in Shipping and Logistics
28. Digital Twins in Maritime: Revolutionizing Asset Management
29. Risk Management in Offshore and Maritime Operations
30. Compliance with IMO 2020 Regulations
31. Sustainable Ship Design: Reducing Environmental Impact
32. Marine Renewable Energy: Wave, Tidal, and Offshore Wind Integration
33. Ballast Water Management Systems
34. Blockchain Technology in Shipping: Improving Transpc'y & Efficiency

35	Effective Supply Chain Management for Energy Industries
36	Leadership in the Energy Transition
37	Effective Crisis Management in Maritime Operations
38	Shipyard Safety Management Systems
39	Port State Control (PSC) Inspection Readiness
40	Remote Vessel Operations and Autonomous Shipping
41	Optimizing Fleet Performance with Data Analytics
42	Maritime Environmental Regulations: Staying Ahead of Compliance
43	Advanced Maintenance Strategies: Condition Monitoring & Pred.Main.
44	Global LNG Market: Trends and Opportunities
45	Incident Investigation in Maritime Operations
46	International Maritime Law: Key Concepts and Applications
47	Emergency Preparedness and Response for Offshore Oil & Gas
48	Energy Transition Strategies for Oil and Gas Companies
49	Maritime Drones: Applications and Safety Considerations
50	Effective Project Management in Offshore Energy Projects

All Rights Reserved Disclaimer

The contents of this book, including but not limited to all text, graphics, images, logos, and designs, are the intellectual property of Gosships LLC and are protected by copyright law. No part of this publication may be reproduced, distributed, transmitted, displayed, or modified in any form or by any means, including photocopying, recording, or other electronic or mechanical methods, without the prior written permission of the publisher, except in the case of brief quotations in critical reviews or articles.

The information contained within this book is for educational purposes only and is provided "as is" without warranty of any kind, either expressed or implied. The authors and publishers disclaim any liability for any direct, indirect, or consequential loss or damage

arising from the use of the material in this book.

For permissions or inquiries, please contact: admin@gosships.com

© 2024 Gosships LLC. All rights reserved.

Chapter 1

Introduction to Hydrogen

Hydrogen is the most abundant element in the universe, making up approximately 75% of all normal matter by mass. It is a simple element, consisting of one proton and one electron. Hydrogen naturally exists as a colorless, odorless, and tasteless gas, and in its molecular form, it is represented as H_2.

Hydrogen has gained significant attention as a clean energy source. Unlike fossil fuels that release carbon dioxide and other pollutants when burned, hydrogen only produces water as a by-product, making it an attractive option for reducing greenhouse gas emissions and combating climate change. It is seen as a crucial component of the energy transition—the global shift from high-carbon energy sources to cleaner, renewable alternatives.

Hydrogen can be used in several sectors, including transportation, industry, and power generation. It is also a flexible energy carrier, capable of being stored and transported, making it ideal for integrating with renewable energy sources like wind and solar, which are intermittent in nature. As the world seeks to reduce its reliance on fossil fuels, hydrogen stands out as a potential game changer in building a sustainable energy future.

Chapter 2

Hydrogen Production Methods

Hydrogen does not naturally exist in large quantities as a free element; it must be produced from compounds that contain hydrogen, such as water or hydrocarbons like natural gas. The methods of hydrogen production can be broadly classified into three categories based on their environmental impact: grey hydrogen, blue hydrogen, and green hydrogen.

Electrolysis

Electrolysis is a process that uses electricity to split water (H_2O) into hydrogen (H_2) and oxygen (O_2). The main advantage of electrolysis is that when the electricity used comes from renewable energy sources, such as wind or solar, the resulting hydrogen is completely carbon-free, known as green hydrogen.

There are several types of electrolysis:

Proton Exchange Membrane (PEM) Electrolysis: A fast and flexible method ideal for pairing with renewable energy sources. It operates at lower temperatures and pressures.

Alkaline Electrolysis: A mature technology that is typically more cost-effective, but less flexible than PEM.

Solid Oxide Electrolysis (SOE): Operates at high temperatures and can potentially achieve higher efficiencies, but is still in the developmental stage.

The scalability of electrolysis is key to its role in the future hydrogen economy, as large-scale deployment could drastically reduce the cost of producing green hydrogen.

Steam Methane Reforming (SMR)

Currently, the most common method of hydrogen production is Steam Methane Reforming (SMR). In this process, natural gas (primarily methane, CH_4) is reacted with steam under high temperature and pressure to produce hydrogen and carbon dioxide. While SMR is efficient and cost-effective, it also results in significant CO_2 emissions. Hydrogen produced through this method is referred to as grey hydrogen.

To mitigate the carbon impact of SMR, blue hydrogen is produced by incorporating carbon capture and storage (CCS) technologies, which capture the CO_2 emissions and store them underground. However, blue hydrogen is still dependent on fossil fuels, and its carbon-neutrality depends on the effectiveness and completeness of the carbon capture process.

Other Methods: Pyrolysis and Biomass Gasification

Pyrolysis: Methane pyrolysis breaks down methane into hydrogen and solid carbon, producing zero CO_2 emissions. Known as turquoise hydrogen, this method is still in its early stages but shows potential for industrial applications.

Biomass Gasification: A process where organic materials like agricultural waste are converted into hydrogen and CO_2, which can be captured and stored, making it another potential source of low-carbon hydrogen.

Chapter 3

Hydrogen Storage and Transport

Hydrogen, despite being the most abundant element, presents several challenges when it comes to storage and transportation. Its low density, both by volume and mass, makes it complex and costly to store and transport in large quantities, requiring innovative solutions for efficient handling.

3.1 Challenges of Storing Hydrogen

Hydrogen is a small molecule and, while it has a high energy density by weight, its low energy density by volume creates significant challenges for storage. Storing hydrogen in sufficient quantities for large-scale applications requires it to be compressed, liquefied, or chemically bound to a carrier. Let's explore the different hydrogen storage methods:

Compressed Gas Storage: This is the most common method of storing hydrogen, where it is compressed at high pressure (typically up to 700 bar) in specialized containers. This method is often used in hydrogen fuel stations and for storage in vehicles, though it requires reinforced tanks, making it less energy-efficient due to the compression energy required.

Liquid Hydrogen Storage: Hydrogen can be stored as a liquid at cryogenic temperatures (around -253°C). Liquid hydrogen has a higher energy density by volume compared to compressed gas, making it more suitable for long-distance transportation. However, liquefaction is energy-intensive and poses challenges related to insulation and boil-off losses, where hydrogen evaporates from the liquid state.

Solid-State Storage: This method involves storing hydrogen in materials like metal hydrides, where hydrogen atoms are chemically absorbed and released from solid compounds.

Although solid-state storage has a high energy density, it is still in developmental stages and faces challenges related to material cost, weight, and efficiency.

3.2 Transporting Hydrogen

Transporting hydrogen is another major challenge in building a hydrogen-based economy. There are several transportation methods:

Pipelines: For short distances, pipelines can be used to transport hydrogen. However, hydrogen's small molecules can cause embrittlement in steel pipelines, necessitating the development of specialized materials or retrofitting existing natural gas pipelines. Currently, only a few regions have dedicated hydrogen pipelines, such as in parts of Europe and the U.S.

Hydrogen Carriers: Hydrogen can be converted into more transportable forms such as ammonia or liquid organic hydrogen carriers (LOHCs). These carriers are easier to handle and transport, as they have higher energy densities and lower storage costs. However, they require additional energy to convert hydrogen back from the carrier form when needed.

Road and Maritime Transport: Hydrogen can also be transported by trucks or ships in compressed or liquefied form. This method is typically used for transporting hydrogen over medium to long distances where pipelines are not feasible, though it is expensive and less efficient than pipeline transport.

Chapter 4

Applications of Hydrogen

Hydrogen is versatile and can be used across several industries, making it a key component in the energy transition. Its uses range from transportation and industrial processes to power generation and residential heating.

4.1 Hydrogen in Transportation

One of the most promising applications of hydrogen is in the transportation sector. Hydrogen Fuel Cell Electric Vehicles (FCEVs) are emerging as a viable alternative to both conventional internal combustion engine vehicles and battery-electric vehicles (BEVs), especially in sectors like heavy-duty transport and long-range travel.

Fuel Cell Electric Vehicles (FCEVs): These vehicles use hydrogen fuel cells to generate electricity on-board, which powers the electric motor. FCEVs offer several advantages over BEVs, including faster refueling times (similar to gasoline vehicles) and longer driving ranges, making them ideal for trucks, buses, and trains.

Hydrogen Trains: Hydrogen-powered trains are already being used in countries like Germany and Japan as alternatives to diesel-powered trains in regions without electrified railways. These trains use hydrogen fuel cells to generate electricity and emit only water vapor, making them an environmentally friendly alternative to traditional trains.

Maritime and Aviation: The use of hydrogen in maritime shipping and aviation is still in its early stages, but it holds promise for reducing emissions in these sectors. In shipping, hydrogen can be used in fuel cells or as ammonia (a hydrogen carrier) in internal combustion engines. In aviation, hydrogen is being explored as a fuel for short-haul flights, either by burning it in modified jet engines or by using fuel cells to power electric planes.

4.2 Hydrogen in Industry

Hydrogen plays a critical role in industrial applications, particularly in sectors that are hard to decarbonize. It is already widely used as a feedstock in industries like refining and ammonia production, but its potential extends to new areas as industries look to decarbonize.

Refining and Ammonia Production: Hydrogen is used in refining processes to remove sulfur from fuels and in ammonia production for fertilizers. Today, most of this hydrogen comes from fossil fuels, making it a significant source of CO_2 emissions. However, transitioning to green hydrogen can reduce the carbon footprint of these industries.

Steel Production: The steel industry is one of the largest carbon emitters, largely due to the use of coal in blast furnaces. Hydrogen-based direct reduction is an emerging technology that uses hydrogen as a reducing agent instead of coal, significantly lowering CO_2 emissions in steelmaking.

Chemical and Petrochemical Industries: Hydrogen is used in various chemical processes, including the production of methanol, which is a key ingredient in plastics, textiles, and pharmaceuticals. By replacing fossil fuel-based hydrogen with green hydrogen, these industries can greatly reduce their carbon footprint.

4.3 Hydrogen in Power Generation

Hydrogen also has the potential to revolutionize power generation, particularly in complementing renewable energy sources like wind and solar.

Fuel Cells for Decentralized Power: Hydrogen fuel cells can be used to generate electricity in off-grid or decentralized power applications. Fuel cells are highly efficient, have low emissions, and are well-suited for backup power systems or remote locations.

Grid Balancing and Energy Storage: One of the biggest challenges with renewable energy sources is their intermittency – wind and solar energy are not always available when needed. Hydrogen can act as an energy storage medium, converting excess renewable energy into hydrogen through electrolysis, which can then be stored and used when demand is high. This concept, known as "power-to-gas," is gaining traction as a way to balance the grid and ensure a reliable supply of electricity.

Co-firing in Natural Gas Plants: Existing natural gas plants can be adapted to co-fire hydrogen alongside natural gas, reducing their carbon emissions. This is seen as a transitional step toward a hydrogen-based power system.

Chapter 5

Environmental and Economic Considerations

Hydrogen has the potential to play a pivotal role in reducing global greenhouse gas emissions, but several environmental and economic factors must be considered for large-scale adoption.

5.1 Environmental Impact of Hydrogen

Hydrogen can significantly reduce CO_2 emissions, but its overall environmental impact depends on how it is produced.

Green Hydrogen: When hydrogen is produced using renewable energy sources (via electrolysis), it is considered "green" hydrogen. Green hydrogen has the potential to nearly eliminate emissions in the sectors where it is used, making it a key part of the global effort to combat climate change.

Grey and Blue Hydrogen: Today, most hydrogen is produced from fossil fuels through steam methane reforming, known as "grey hydrogen." This process emits significant amounts of CO_2, making it unsuitable for a low-carbon future. However, "blue hydrogen" uses carbon capture and storage (CCS) technology to capture most of these emissions, making it a cleaner alternative.

5.2 Economic Viability of Hydrogen

While hydrogen holds great promise, its economic viability remains a major challenge. The cost of producing green hydrogen is still significantly higher than fossil fuel-based hydrogen, though costs are expected to decrease as renewable energy prices fall and electrolyzer technology improves.

Current Costs: Green hydrogen currently costs between $4-6 per kilogram, whereas grey hydrogen costs about $1-2 per kilogram. However, the gap is expected to narrow as investments in green hydrogen production increase and economies of scale are realized.

Infrastructure Investment: Developing the infrastructure needed for hydrogen storage, transportation, and refueling is costly and will require significant investment from both the public and private sectors. Governments around the world are starting to invest in hydrogen infrastructure, offering subsidies and incentives to accelerate its development.

Chapter 6

Hydrogen Safety

While hydrogen offers many benefits, there are also safety concerns related to its use, storage, and transportation.

6.1 Hydrogen Safety Concerns

Hydrogen is highly flammable, and its small molecules can easily leak from storage containers, posing risks in certain environments.

Flammability: Hydrogen has a wide flammability range, meaning it can ignite in relatively low concentrations in air. This requires careful handling and storage to prevent leaks and minimize the risk of explosions.

Leakage: Hydrogen's small molecular size means it can leak from storage tanks and pipelines more easily than other gases. To address this, safety protocols and advanced materials are used in hydrogen systems to minimize leakage.

6.2 Advancements in Hydrogen Safety

Recent advancements in materials science and safety protocols are improving the safety of hydrogen systems.

New Materials: Researchers are developing advanced materials that are more resistant to hydrogen embrittlement, making pipelines and storage tanks safer. For example, new composite materials are being developed for high-pressure hydrogen storage tanks that are more durable and less prone to leaks.

Safety Protocols: Strict safety standards and protocols are in place for hydrogen systems. These include regular inspections, leak detection systems, and emergency response procedures to mitigate the risks associated with hydrogen use.

Chapter 7

Hydrogen Fuel Cells

Hydrogen fuel cells are a crucial technology that can convert hydrogen directly into electricity with high efficiency and minimal environmental impact. They have a wide range of applications, including in transportation, power generation, and industrial sectors, positioning them as a cornerstone for the future hydrogen economy.

7.1 How Hydrogen Fuel Cells Work

At their core, hydrogen fuel cells generate electricity through a chemical reaction between hydrogen and oxygen, producing only water and heat as byproducts. The basic components of a fuel cell include the anode, cathode, and electrolyte membrane.

At the Anode, hydrogen molecules are split into protons and electrons. This process is facilitated by a catalyst (often platinum). The protons move through the electrolyte membrane toward the cathode, while the electrons flow through an external circuit, creating an electric current.

At the Cathode, the protons and electrons recombine with oxygen to produce water and release heat. This makes hydrogen fuel cells extremely clean, as the only emissions are water vapor.

The overall reaction is: $2H_2 + O_2 \rightarrow 2H_2O + \text{electricity} + \text{heat}$

Fuel cells operate continuously as long as hydrogen and oxygen are supplied, making them a reliable and scalable energy source.

7.2 Types of Hydrogen Fuel Cells

There are several types of hydrogen fuel cells, each optimized for different applications based on temperature, efficiency, and scalability. The two most common types are Proton Exchange Membrane (PEM) and Solid Oxide Fuel Cells (SOFC).

Proton Exchange Membrane (PEM) Fuel Cells: These are the most commonly used fuel cells in transportation applications. PEM fuel cells operate at relatively low temperatures (60-80°C), making them ideal for vehicles, including cars, buses, and trucks. They are lightweight, have quick start-up times, and offer good power-to-weight ratios, essential for automotive use.

Solid Oxide Fuel Cells (SOFC): These fuel cells operate at much higher temperatures (500-1,000°C) and are more suited for stationary power generation. SOFCs can run on various fuels (including hydrogen, natural gas, and biofuels) and have higher efficiency rates than PEM fuel cells, especially in combined heat and power (CHP) applications.

Other types of fuel cells include Alkaline Fuel Cells (AFC), used in space exploration, and Molten Carbonate Fuel Cells (MCFC), used in large-scale power generation.

7.3 Applications of Hydrogen Fuel Cells

Fuel cells are emerging as a versatile solution for both mobile and stationary applications.

Transportation: Hydrogen fuel cells are gaining traction in the automotive sector. Fuel cell electric vehicles (FCEVs) can be refueled in just minutes and offer longer ranges than battery electric vehicles (BEVs), especially in heavy-duty transport such as trucks, buses, and trains. In aviation, hydrogen fuel cells are being explored as a potential power source for short-haul flights, while maritime industries are investigating fuel cells for zero-emission shipping.

Stationary Power Generation: Hydrogen fuel cells are well-suited for decentralized power generation, particularly in remote areas or locations without access to the electrical grid. They are also used in backup power systems for data centers, hospitals, and critical infrastructure, where reliability and quick start-up are essential.

Portable Power: Fuel cells are also being used in smaller-scale applications, such as portable chargers, drones, and military equipment, where lightweight, long-lasting energy sources are required.

Chapter 8

Hydrogen's Role in the Energy Transition

Hydrogen is expected to play a critical role in the global energy transition as countries and industries work toward decarbonization and the adoption of cleaner energy sources. By integrating hydrogen with renewable energy systems, it can provide flexibility, storage, and long-term solutions for sectors that are difficult to decarbonize.

8.1 Hydrogen as a Renewable Energy Storage Solution

One of the biggest challenges with renewable energy sources like wind and solar is their intermittency. These energy sources do not produce electricity continuously and can fluctuate depending on weather conditions or time of day. Hydrogen offers a promising solution for storing excess renewable energy and ensuring a consistent supply.

Power-to-Gas Systems: When renewable energy generation exceeds demand, the excess electricity can be used to produce hydrogen via electrolysis. This hydrogen can then be stored and used later when renewable energy production is low, either for electricity generation (through fuel cells) or as fuel for industrial processes.

Grid Balancing: Hydrogen can help balance electrical grids by absorbing excess energy during periods of high renewable generation and releasing it when demand spikes. This helps prevent blackouts and ensures that renewable energy is used efficiently, reducing the need for fossil fuel-powered backup systems.

8.2 Decarbonizing Hard-to-Abate Sectors

While renewable electricity can decarbonize many sectors, certain industries are difficult to electrify due to their high energy demands or technical constraints. Hydrogen is expected to play a major role in decarbonizing these hard-to-abate sectors, including heavy industry, shipping, and aviation.

Heavy Industry: Industries like steel, cement, and chemicals are responsible for significant carbon emissions, as they rely heavily on fossil fuels for heat and energy. Hydrogen can serve as both a fuel and feedstock in these industries, reducing or even eliminating CO_2 emissions. For example, hydrogen-based direct reduction in steelmaking is an emerging technology that uses hydrogen instead of coal to produce steel with lower emissions.

Shipping and Aviation: These sectors are particularly challenging to decarbonize because of the energy density required for long-distance travel. Hydrogen can be used in fuel cells or as a combustible fuel in modified engines for aircraft and ships. Additionally, hydrogen-derived fuels like ammonia and synthetic fuels can be used as drop-in replacements for fossil fuels in existing engines, offering a pathway to decarbonization without requiring major changes to infrastructure.

Chapter 9

Global Initiatives and Hydrogen Policy

Countries around the world are investing in hydrogen as part of their clean energy strategies, recognizing its potential to meet both climate goals and energy security needs. Governments and private companies are developing roadmaps, policies, and initiatives to promote the adoption of hydrogen technology.

9.1 Hydrogen Roadmaps by Region

Several regions have established ambitious hydrogen strategies to accelerate the development of hydrogen infrastructure and technologies.

European Union: The EU has adopted a Hydrogen Strategy that aims to produce 10 million tons of renewable hydrogen by 2030, with plans to scale up electrolyzer capacity and develop cross-border hydrogen infrastructure. Hydrogen is seen as key to achieving the EU's climate neutrality target by 2050.

Japan: Japan has been a leader in hydrogen technology for decades, pioneering fuel cell development and promoting the use of hydrogen in transportation and energy storage. Japan's Basic Hydrogen Strategy aims to establish a full hydrogen supply chain by 2030, with plans to develop hydrogen imports, domestic production, and distribution networks.

United States: The U.S. is focusing on hydrogen as a way to decarbonize its industrial sector and reduce reliance on fossil fuels. The Department of Energy's Hydrogen Earthshot initiative seeks to lower the cost of clean hydrogen production to $1 per kilogram within the next decade, making it competitive with other energy sources.

South Korea: South Korea's hydrogen strategy includes plans to build a hydrogen-based society by 2040, with ambitious targets for hydrogen fuel cell vehicles, refueling stations, and green hydrogen production.

9.2 Public-Private Partnerships and Hydrogen Alliances

Collaboration between governments, private companies, and research institutions is critical to the success of the global hydrogen economy. Public-private partnerships are helping to fund hydrogen infrastructure projects and promote technology innovation.

The Hydrogen Council: This global initiative brings together CEOs from leading companies in the energy, transportation, and industrial sectors to accelerate the deployment of hydrogen solutions. The council works to create a roadmap for scaling up hydrogen technologies and encourages investment in hydrogen infrastructure.

Mission Innovation's Hydrogen Valley Platform: This initiative supports the development of hydrogen valleys – regional hubs where hydrogen production, storage, and usage are concentrated to create self-sustaining ecosystems. Hydrogen valleys help demonstrate the viability of hydrogen technologies and reduce costs through economies of scale.

Chapter 10

The Future of Hydrogen

Hydrogen is emerging as one of the most promising energy carriers of the future. As industries and governments around the world look for ways to reduce carbon emissions and move toward cleaner energy systems, hydrogen stands out as a versatile and scalable solution. In this chapter, we will explore hydrogen's long-term potential, emerging technologies, and the challenges ahead.

10.1 Long-Term Vision for Hydrogen

The transition to a hydrogen-based economy has the potential to revolutionize how we produce, store, and use energy. Hydrogen is expected to play a central role in decarbonizing hard-to-abate sectors, including industries like steel, cement, shipping, and aviation, which are difficult to electrify directly with renewable energy.

Industry Decarbonization: Hydrogen has the potential to replace fossil fuels in industrial processes where electrification is not feasible. For example, hydrogen can be used in steel production to replace coal in the blast furnace, dramatically reducing carbon emissions. Other industries, such as chemicals and refining, are also looking at hydrogen as a clean alternative to traditional fuels and feedstocks.

Transportation: Hydrogen fuel cell electric vehicles (FCEVs) are poised to expand beyond cars into larger transport sectors such as trucks, buses, trains, and even planes. As infrastructure develops and hydrogen costs decrease, hydrogen-powered transportation could provide a zero-emission solution for long-range, heavy-duty applications where batteries are less effective.

Energy Storage and Grid Balancing: Hydrogen can act as a large-scale energy storage medium, converting excess renewable energy into hydrogen during times of low demand and storing it for later use. This could help balance the grid, ensuring a reliable supply of energy even when the sun isn't shining or the wind isn't blowing. Hydrogen's role as an energy storage solution is essential for integrating high shares of renewable energy into the global energy mix.

Distributed and Remote Energy: Hydrogen offers an opportunity for decentralized power generation, especially in remote or off-grid areas. Hydrogen fuel cells can be deployed where traditional energy infrastructure is lacking, providing reliable, clean energy to regions that currently depend on diesel generators or other fossil fuel-based power.

As countries pursue net-zero emission goals, hydrogen will likely account for a significant share of global energy demand by 2050. The transition to hydrogen will not only help decarbonize various sectors but also improve energy security, enabling countries to diversify their energy supplies and reduce reliance on imported fossil fuels.

10.2 Emerging Technologies in Hydrogen

While hydrogen already shows great potential, continued research and innovation will be key to addressing current challenges and making hydrogen more accessible and cost-effective. Several emerging technologies are expected to shape the future of the hydrogen economy:

Advanced Electrolyzers: Electrolyzers are central to producing green hydrogen through water electrolysis powered by renewable energy. Advances in solid oxide electrolyzers (SOE) and high-temperature systems promise to significantly improve efficiency. These new technologies could make green hydrogen cheaper by reducing the electricity required for electrolysis. Integration with industrial processes to use waste heat could further enhance their efficiency.

Hydrogen Fuel Cells: Fuel cells, which convert hydrogen into electricity, continue to evolve, with new designs improving efficiency, durability, and scalability. Next-generation fuel cells are being designed for large-scale applications such as shipping, aviation, and grid-level power generation. These fuel cells will be crucial for sectors where battery storage alone may not be practical.

Solid-State Hydrogen Storage: Traditional methods of hydrogen storage, such as compression and liquefaction, have limitations in terms of energy efficiency and cost. Solid-state storage methods, such as metal hydrides, are emerging as a promising alternative. These materials can absorb and release hydrogen, offering higher energy densities and safer storage options. Although still in development, solid-state hydrogen storage could become a game-changer for both stationary and mobile hydrogen applications.

Hydrogen Blending: One interim solution being explored is blending hydrogen with natural gas in existing pipelines. This allows countries to begin reducing their reliance on fossil fuels without requiring a complete overhaul of infrastructure. Over time, the proportion of hydrogen in the blend can increase, eventually phasing out natural gas entirely.

Hydrogen Carriers: Transporting hydrogen in its pure form can be costly and inefficient due to its low density. Hydrogen carriers, such as ammonia and liquid organic hydrogen carriers (LOHCs), offer a way to transport hydrogen more efficiently over long distances. Ammonia, for instance, can be used as both a carrier and a fuel in itself, making it an attractive option for international shipping and energy exports.

10.3 Challenges Ahead

While hydrogen holds enormous promise, several challenges remain that must be addressed for it to achieve its full potential in the global energy mix.

Cost of Green Hydrogen: Although costs for green hydrogen are falling, they remain significantly higher than for hydrogen produced from fossil fuels (grey and blue hydrogen). Scaling up production capacity, improving electrolyzer efficiency, and reducing renewable electricity costs are essential to making green hydrogen cost-competitive.

Infrastructure Development: Developing a global hydrogen infrastructure will require significant investment. This includes building hydrogen production facilities, storage systems, pipelines, refueling stations, and export terminals. Governments and the private sector must work together to finance and build the necessary infrastructure to support a hydrogen-based economy.

Policy and Regulation: Clear policy frameworks and supportive regulations are needed to incentivize the adoption of hydrogen technology. Governments must provide consistent and stable policies that promote investment in hydrogen production and infrastructure, while also setting standards for safety and emissions reductions. International cooperation will be essential to harmonize regulations and create a global market for hydrogen.

Technological Scaling: Many hydrogen technologies, such as advanced fuel cells and solid-state storage, are still in the developmental or pilot stages. Significant research and development efforts are needed to scale these technologies for mass adoption. Furthermore, global supply chains for critical materials like platinum (used in fuel cells) and rare earth elements (used in electrolyzers) must be expanded to support widespread hydrogen deployment.

Public Perception and Safety: Hydrogen, despite its potential benefits, faces challenges related to public perception and safety concerns. Hydrogen is highly flammable, and incidents like the Hindenburg disaster have left a lasting negative impression. While modern hydrogen storage and handling technologies are safe and well-regulated, educating the public and ensuring confidence in hydrogen's safety will be critical to its widespread acceptance.

10.4 The Road Ahead

The next decade will be pivotal for the hydrogen economy. Countries and companies are already making significant investments in hydrogen technologies, and global initiatives like the Hydrogen Council and Mission Innovation are accelerating progress. However, achieving a sustainable hydrogen economy will require continued collaboration between governments, industries, and research institutions.

Collaboration and Partnerships: International cooperation is key to accelerating hydrogen deployment. Governments must collaborate to establish global hydrogen trade routes, while public-private partnerships can help build the infrastructure and scale up production. Major energy companies are already forming alliances with technology providers, utilities, and automakers to develop integrated hydrogen ecosystems.

Decentralized Production: Hydrogen's future could involve more localized production, particularly in regions rich in renewable resources. This would reduce transportation costs and energy losses associated with long-distance hydrogen transport, making it more efficient and affordable.

Hydrogen Valleys: A promising approach to scaling up hydrogen deployment is the concept of hydrogen valleys – regional clusters where hydrogen production, storage, and usage are concentrated. These hubs create economies of scale, allowing hydrogen technologies to be developed, tested, and deployed in a real-world setting. Over time, these valleys could expand into larger hydrogen corridors, connecting different regions and industries.

10.5 Hydrogen's Role in a Carbon-Free Future

In the quest to decarbonize the global economy, hydrogen stands out as a versatile and essential fuel. Its ability to integrate with renewable energy systems, decarbonize hard-to-abate sectors, and provide a clean fuel for transportation and industry makes it a cornerstone of future energy strategies.

While the challenges are significant, the momentum behind hydrogen continues to grow, driven by advancements in technology, policy support, and increasing awareness of the urgent need to address climate change. With continued innovation and collaboration, hydrogen has the potential to unlock a cleaner, more sustainable future.

Conclusion

Hydrogen is no longer a distant dream for the future – it is rapidly becoming a reality, poised to transform energy systems around the world. As nations strive to meet ambitious climate goals and industries seek cleaner alternatives, hydrogen's versatility, scalability, and potential for deep decarbonization make it an indispensable part of the global energy transition.

Through advancements in production, storage, and application technologies, hydrogen is well-positioned to revolutionize industries, enable the large-scale adoption of renewable energy, and help build a cleaner, greener world. The road ahead for hydrogen is long, but the foundation is being laid for a future where hydrogen is the fuel that powers our economy and preserves our planet for generations to come.

Glossary

Alkaline Electrolysis: A cost-effective electrolysis method for hydrogen production.

Ammonia (NH_3): A hydrogen carrier that can be used for easier transport and as fuel.

Biomass Gasification: Producing hydrogen from organic materials like agricultural waste.

Blue Hydrogen: Hydrogen produced from natural gas with carbon capture and storage to reduce emissions.

Carbon Capture and Storage (CCS): Technology to capture CO_2 emissions from hydrogen production, storing them underground.

Compressed Hydrogen Storage: Hydrogen stored under high pressure in reinforced tanks. Electrolysis: Method using electricity to split water into hydrogen and oxygen, producing green hydrogen when powered by renewables.

Decarbonization: Reducing carbon emissions through cleaner energy sources, including hydrogen.

Fuel Cell: A device that converts hydrogen into electricity, used in transport and power generation.

Green Hydrogen: Hydrogen produced using renewable energy, carbon-free.

Grey Hydrogen: Hydrogen produced from natural gas without capturing emissions, contributing to CO_2 emissions.

Hydrogen (H_2): The most abundant element, used in clean energy, producing water as a by-product, crucial for decarbonization.

Hydrogen Economy: An energy system where hydrogen is a primary energy source, reducing reliance on fossil fuels.

Hydrogen Embrittlement: The weakening of materials, especially metals, caused by exposure to hydrogen.

Hydrogen Fuel Cell Electric Vehicles (FCEVs): Vehicles powered by hydrogen fuel cells, producing only water as emissions.

Hydrogen Pipeline: Pipelines transporting hydrogen, requiring special materials due to hydrogen's properties.

Hydrogen Trains: Trains powered by hydrogen fuel cells, reducing emissions in non-electrified railways.

Hydrogen Valley: A regional hub focusing on hydrogen production, storage, and use for integrated solutions.

Liquid Hydrogen Storage: Storing hydrogen as a liquid at cryogenic temperatures for long-distance transport.

Power-to-Gas (PtG): Converting excess renewable energy into hydrogen for storage and later use.

Proton Exchange Membrane (PEM): A type of electrolysis and fuel cell technology, ideal for transport.

Pyrolysis: The thermal decomposition of methane to produce hydrogen and solid carbon, without CO_2 emissions.

Renewable Energy: Energy from natural sources like wind or solar, used for hydrogen production.

Solid Oxide Electrolysis (SOE): High-efficiency hydrogen production method, still in development.

Steam Methane Reforming (SMR): The process of producing hydrogen from methane, emitting CO_2.

www.ingramcontent.com/pod-product-compliance
Lightning Source LLC
Chambersburg PA
CBHW030105230526
45471CB00003B/1263